HALLEY: COMET 1986

ALSO BY FRANKLYN M. BRANLEY

FRANKLYN M. BRANLEY

HALLEY: COMET 1986

DIAGRAMS BY

SALLY J. BENSUSEN

LODESTAR BOOKS

E. P. Dutton   New York

LIBRARY OF CONGRESS CATALOGING IN PUBLICATION DATA
Branley, Franklyn Mansfield, date.
    Halley: comet 1986.
    Bibliography: p.
    Includes index.
    Summary: Describes the sightings of Halley's
comet throughout history and how its movements were
definitively charted by the astronomer whose
name it bears. Also discusses the composition of
comets and their relationship to the earth, other
famous comets, and the return of Halley's comet in
1986.
    1. Halley's comet—Juvenile literature.
[1. Halley's comet.   2. Comets]
I. Bensusen, Sally, ill.   II. Title.
QB723.H2B73   1982   523.6   82-9919
ISBN 0-525-66780-6   AACR2

Published in the United States by E. P. Dutton
2 Park Avenue, New York, N.Y. 10016

EDITOR: Virginia Buckley   DESIGNER: Trish Parcell

Printed in the U.S.A.
10 9 8 7 6 5 4

CONTENTS

Edmund Halley (1656–1742) left school at age twenty to become an astronomer. Later he became the Astronomer Royal of England. In 1705 he predicted
the return in 1758 of a comet that he had seen in 1682. When it appeared as
he had said it would, Halley's name was given to the comet.

Early Appearances

In late 1985 and the early part of 1986, you will be able to see Halley's comet. Right now it is moving toward us. In October 1982, astronomers sighted it, a small object more than a billion kilometers away. Down through history it has been appearing about every 76 years.

The comet is named after Edmund Halley, an English astronomer who watched it during its appearance in 1682. After watching it, he worked out how the comet moves. This enabled him to predict it would reappear in 1758. And it did. It was Edmund Halley who gave us much knowledge of the movements of comets.

Strangely enough, sixteen hundred years before Edmund Halley was born, Lucius Seneca, a Roman philosopher, said, "Someday there will arise a man who will demonstrate in what region of the heavens the comets take their way; why they journey so far apart from the other planets; what their size, their nature."

It's curious that he could have been so correct. That man turned out to be Edmund Halley.

His comet is among the most famous of all, for if you asked people to name a comet, this is the one that would be mentioned most often. And in the entire solar system—the Sun, the nine planets and their dozens of satellites, the meteors and asteroids—Halley's comet, it seems to many, is very important.

Because of its regular appearances, Halley has been called a sort of clock that counts time in human lifetimes. Your great-grandparents, or your grandparents, if they are quite old, may have told you about Halley's visit in 1910. And you may tell your own grandchildren about the comet of 1986. Once every 76 years, many people who have lived on Earth during the past two or three thousand years have had the chance to see Halley.

The comet marked the beginning and end of the life of Samuel Clemens (Mark Twain), the author of *Tom Sawyer* and *Huckleberry Finn*. The comet appeared in 1835, when Mark Twain was born, and it reappeared in 1910, when he died at the age of seventy-five.

In 87 B.C., when he was thirteen years old, Julius Caesar saw it. In A.D. 1066, over a thousand years later, the same comet was seen by Harold, king of England. Edmund Halley saw it in 1682.

In 1986 you will be able to see Halley's comet, too. You might even see it again in 2062, when it will make another return visit to our region of the solar system.

Because Halley told us the time between visits, and where the comet can be seen, astronomers can pretty well tell whether or not a comet is Halley's. When historical reports of comets—that is, the time a comet appeared and its location—are reliable, astronomers can be quite certain the comet was Halley's.

Since 239 B.C., Halley's comet (pronounced HAL-ee) has returned every 75 to 79 years, averaging close to every 76 years. Chinese astronomers believe they can trace the comet back to 1057 B.C. Because of confusion about dates that long ago, however, not all people agree the comet seen then was Halley. They say that the oldest fairly reliable date for the sighting of Halley, and for which there are enough records of its location, is probably 467 B.C. Accounts of sightings that long ago are scarce. And even when there are reports, we cannot be sure that the comet described was Halley. It could have been some other comet that arrived around the time and place of Halley's expected appearance.

However, occasionally there are records that set the dates very accurately. One of these is the Bayeux tapestry. It is a pictorial history woven a few years after 1066, the year when the Normans invaded England. The tapestry, 70 meters long and 50 centimeters wide, is woven with wool on linen cloth. It was made at the request of the brother of William, the successful leader of the invasion, to be hung in the cathedral at Bayeux in French Normandy. The tapestry pictures the history of the conquest, and one of the panels shows a comet—Halley—during its appearance in April of 1066.

The weavers of the tapestry showed the alarm of the people as they pointed toward the comet. Included is a picture of King Harold of England, who appears quite disturbed. In those days, comets were believed to foretell events, especially calamities of one kind or another, and this one was supposed to have contributed to Harold's defeat. The comet's effects are still remembered today, for the crown of the king of England contains a jewel that represents it.

Earlier, in 837, a comet appeared during the reign of Louis I the Pious, also called the Debonair, in France. From the report of it, you can see that comets were not welcome sights.

Halley, as shown in this section of the Bayeux tapestry, was supposed to have foretold the defeat of King Harold of England. Here his subjects show alarm at the sight of the comet.   Yerkes Observatory photograph

During the holy days of Easter, a phenomenon which is always ominous and a carrier of bad news appeared in the sky. As soon as the emperor, who always paid great attention to such events, had noticed it, he allowed himself no rest. The king believed that a change of reign and the death of a prince are announced by this sign. He consulted the bishops, who advised him to pray, build churches, and found monasteries, which he did. But he died three years later.

Even though a comet might appear years before, or after, a disaster, it was still believed to have caused the event. Because of the time of its arrival and its position, astronomers are sure that this comet of 837 was another appearance of Halley.

Another famous appearance of Halley's comet occurred in 1456, three years after the Turks captured Constantinople (Istanbul). This was during a terrible religious war that was raging between the Muslims and Christians. The Muslims had won one victory after another, and they were then attacking Belgrade in Serbia (Yugoslavia). Christians there were slaughtered, and people throughout Europe trembled in fear. The comet made matters worse. It was like a flame, considered a sign of divine anger, and it added to the terrors of that war, which had been raging for several years. People were told to pray for deliverance. The pope required that bells be rung at noon, and that people pray at that time as well as at other times of the day. The noon Angelus (prayer) dates from 1456, the year of the comet's appearance. In 1472 King Louis XI made noonday prayers a regular French custom.

Through the years Halley has reappeared dozens of times. At the time of many of the appearances, calamities of some kind or other—wars, famines, floods, the death of rulers—seem to have occurred. It is easy to see why people who were superstitious believed that the comet in some way caused these disasters.

A few appearances of Halley are listed below:

1986 The first of what may be two sightings during your lifetime.

1910 Earth passes through the tail of the comet. No effects are noted.

1835 A plague sweeps through Egypt, causing widespread death.

1758 Halley predicted this return, but he did not live to see it happen.

1682 Halley studies the appearance and motion of the planet. Later he is to determine its path through the solar system.

1607 Johannes Kepler, a famous German astronomer, attempts to determine the path of the comet.

1531 Halley's investigations convince him that this comet, and the one that appeared in 1607, are the same as the comet he saw in 1682.

1456 The time of the great war between the Christians and the Muslims. People pray to be saved from "the devil, the Turks, and the Comet."

1222 Genghis Khan, a powerful Mongol leader who has a tremendous army, takes the comet as a sign to conquer the world.

1066 The Normans invade England. King Harold, seeing the comet, believes he is doomed to defeat.

837 King Louis I of France dies three years after the comet appeared.

684 A plague spreads across China, killing hundreds of thousands.

530 A plague spreads across Europe, believed to be caused by the comet.

A.D.66 The city of Jerusalem is attacked by the Romans.

87B.C. At the age of thirteen, Julius Caesar sees Halley.

239 In March of that year, Halley sweeps around the Sun. One of the earliest reliable sightings of the comet.

1057 Chinese astronomers may have seen Halley. However, astronomers question whether this comet is actually Halley.

2 Comets—Evil Stars

People of long ago—until after the Middle Ages—were frightened by the appearance of any comet, not only Halley's.

The word *comet* comes from the Greek *kometes,* meaning hairy. Comets were known as *kometes asters*—hairy stars, or, more usually, long-haired stars, because of their long tails. They were also called *dis asters,* or evil stars. People were terrified by them, for they imagined they saw fiery swords, bloodstained crosses, armies of soldiers, dragons, or flaming daggers in the comets.

Even educated people feared them. In 1577, after seeing a comet, a French physician wrote,

This comet was so horrible and terrifying, and it aroused such fear among the populace, that some died of fright as a result, while others fell ill. It appeared to be exceedingly long and was of the color of blood; at the top the figure of a bent arm was visible, holding a great sword in its hand as though about to strike. At the point of the sword there were three stars. At the two sides of the rays of this comet, there were seen a great number of axes, knives, and bloodstained swords, among which were many hideous human faces with their beards and hairs standing on end.

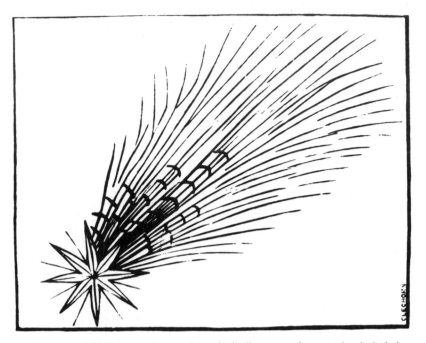

A drawing of Halley, made in 684, which illustrates the popular belief that comets were long-haired stars.   Yerkes Observatory photograph

Comets were also believed to be omens of events to come, and, invariably, they were associated with the death of a ruler, of someone in high places. In his play *Julius Caesar*, Shakespeare wrote, "When beggars die, there are no comets seen; The heavens themselves blaze forth the deaths of princes."

Even if a comet's appearance occurred a few years earlier or later than the death of a prince or king, people related the two events. The deaths of many great men were connected with comets: Constantine, Attila the Hun, the Islamic prophet Muhammad, Louis I of France, Pope Alexander III, and others.

The worst calamity that could occur would be the collision of a comet with the Earth. If it ever happened, there would be widespread destruction, perhaps the end of the

As depicted in this drawing made in 1520, comets were considered omens of wars to come, defeats to be suffered, and the deaths of kings and rulers.

Comets were horrors, thought to foretell war and devastation. They were called *dis asters,* meaning evil stars.

world. In 1758 people were fearful about the return of Halley's comet. John Wesley, a famous English churchman and preacher, expressed everyone's feelings when he warned his followers about the comet. He said, "Were it to hit upon the Earth—when it is some one thousand times hotter than a red-hot cannonball, who does not see what must be the immediate consequence?"

Immediately, people imagined all sorts of calamities. Whether or not it could actually happen, people were frightened by the prediction. Fortunately, there was no collision in 1758. But they still remembered the words of John Wesley in 1773, a few years later, when another comet was seen. In Paris people were scared by rumors that the comet would destroy the Earth on May 20 of that year.

They demanded that their mayors go to the archbishop requesting that he pray to God to change the path of the comet from a collision course. Once again, there was no catastrophe, and this time, no doubt, many believed that disaster was averted only because of the prayers.

Beliefs in the evil nature of comets were completely unfounded. However, there was some basis for the belief that a comet might collide with the Earth. In 1832 observers predicted that Biela, a small comet, would pass through Earth's orbit on October 29. When the public learned of this, there was panic. Many thought it meant there would be a collision, and the world would be shattered.

But the story in the newspapers left out one important piece of information: Where would Earth be when the comet passed through its orbit? Astronomers worked out the position of Earth on October 29 and found that it would arrive at the location one day later, on October 30.

The comet and Earth would be thousands of kilometers apart, and so there was no cause for alarm. Even so, many were not convinced, and the panic continued until long after the visit of Biela's comet.

Yet there actually may have been collisions and near collisions during Earth's history. Sixty-five million years ago a comet may have collided with Earth. If so, it would

Sixty-five million years ago there may have been a comet collision, *top left*. A near miss, *top right*, would create massive meteor showers, and perhaps darken the sky. In 1910, Earth passed through the tail of Halley with no effect, in spite of warnings poisons would rain down on us, *bottom*.

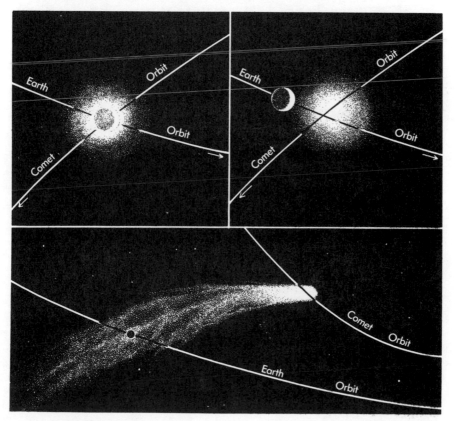

help explain the disappearance of the dinosaurs. Dust from the comet and ash from the crater it made in the Earth would have been held in the air. It would have spread all around the Earth, a great cloud that filtered out sunlight. Because only a small amount of sunlight could penetrate this cloud, the temperature of the world would have dropped considerably. Plants could not flourish, and so, lacking food, dinosaurs would have disappeared. There is little evidence to prove this belief, no craters or other signs of a collision; still, it is possible that such a chain of events did occur.

In 1908 a tremendous bright light was seen over the skies of the Tunguska Plateau in Siberia, Russia. There were deafening booms, and the ground shook. The region is desolate, and in 1908 it was difficult to reach. However, when scientists finally got there, they found that the trees for kilometers around had been laid flat, and they all were in positions pointing away from the point of impact. Hundreds of small craters were found. Many scientists believe that a small comet caused the destruction, which, when it was a few kilometers above Earth, exploded into many separate pieces. This would explain the hundreds of small craters, the flattened trees, the shaking ground, the loud noise, and the blinding light that was seen from far away. Perhaps that is really what happened, so we can't blame people for having been frightened by John Wesley's warning in 1758 or by the approach of a comet in 1773.

We can understand why people have been frightened by comets. Except for rare eclipses that darkened the Sun, the sky and the objects in it were constant and reliable. The planets moved in predictable ways, the Moon went through regular changes, the Sun, Moon, and stars rose and set. But comets loomed suddenly into the sky, seeming to appear from nowhere. They hung over the Earth, their long tails making them appear to be fingers of fate pointing toward the people and warning them of disasters. And then, just as suddenly as they appeared, they were gone. People did not understand comets, and so they attached all sorts of mystical powers to them.

Such attitudes were to change as people gradually learned what comets were, how they moved, and where they came from.

3 Dirty Snowballs

It has been said that comets are about as close to nothing as something can get. During the visit of Halley's comet in 1910, it developed a tail that was 240 million kilometers long. Yet the core of the comet—the main part—is probably only 5 kilometers across. The particles in the central part of a comet are so widely separated that it is 10 trillion (ten thousand billion) times less dense than air. In fact, it is so empty that a molecule could travel 1 000 kilometers before striking another one. (At sea level on Earth, a molecule can move only .0001 millimeter without colliding.) In the tail of a comet, a molecule could travel well over a million kilometers without contacting another one.

The three main parts of a comet are the tail (that's the part most often seen from Earth); the coma, or region where the tail seems to originate and which may be 150 000 kilometers across; and the nucleus, a small, more tightly packed region at the center of the coma. The nucleus is so small that it cannot be seen from Earth. In Halley's comet it weighs some 65 billion tons and rotates once in a little over ten hours. About 40 percent of it consists of frozen materials in the form of water-ice, and some

10 percent is in the form of solids that become methane, ammonia, hydrogen, and other gases as the comet nears the Sun. The rest of the core is composed of solid substances, probably dust and stony material much like fine sand.

In the 1950s it was suggested that the nucleus of a comet is made up of water-ice and solids mixed together; that it is something like a dirty snowball. There are many who support this theory. Certainly when the light of a comet is analyzed, one of the materials identified is water. And because a comet's interior is very cold, the water would be frozen solid. During most of their existence, comets are dark, frigid cosmic snowballs. They become visible only when they are near the Sun. Then parts of the nucleus become gases, and a coma develops. The coma becomes larger; it reflects more sunlight and so it becomes brighter. As the comet moves away from the Sun, less light is reflected. The comet grows dimmer until finally it can no longer be seen from Earth.

4 Comet Jets and Comet Tails

Comets do not always behave as predicted. For example, they may be speeded up or slowed down by the attraction or repulsion of planets. In Halley's day a comet might appear several months earlier or later than predicted. That was because in those days astronomers did not know there were other planets out there beyond Saturn—Uranus, Neptune, and Pluto had not yet been discovered. Depending on the locations of those planets in relation to the path of the comet, their gravitations may have speeded up or slowed down the comet.

Even today, comets do not always arrive on time, but the delay is now measured in hours rather than in weeks or months. They may be two or three hours early or late. It would seem that a few hours one way or another would make little difference, and they don't. But astronomers cannot accept such variations. They must have explanations for them.

It has been suggested that when a comet approaches the Sun, its Sun side heats up. Bits of ice in the nucleus change to gas, which is then ejected in what is called a comet jet. This jet causes the comet to move in the di-

16

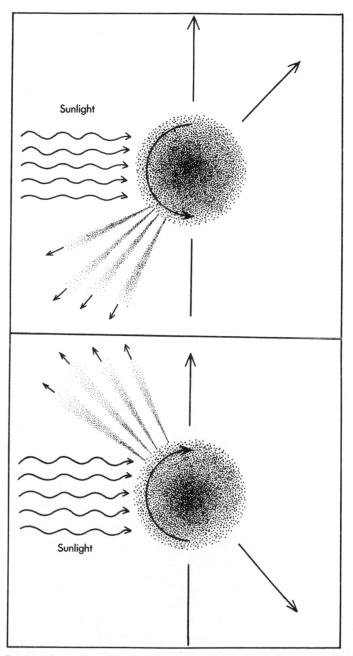

As Halley's nucleus nears the Sun, gases will jet from the nucleus. This will cause a jet reaction. If the nucleus is spinning counterclockwise, the reaction will push the nucleus outward, slowing the comet. Should the nucleus spin clockwise, the jet reaction causes the nucleus to drift inward, speeding up the comet.

rection opposite to that of the jet. For example, if the gas is ejected to the right, the nucleus moves to the left. At the same time that the jet is operating, the comet is rotating: The core of most comets spins constantly. If the rotation is in the same direction as the comet's motion around the Sun, the reaction will push the nucleus away from the Sun. This will cause the comet to move more slowly; the farther it is pushed from the Sun, the slower it moves. Since it will move more slowly than usual, it will appear later than expected.

Should the nucleus be spinning opposite to its motion in orbit, the nucleus will react to the jet by moving into an orbit that is closer to the Sun. This speeds up the comet, causing it to appear a few hours earlier than predicted. The direction of spin of comets is random: About half rotate in a direction that is the same as the direction around the Sun, and half rotate in the opposite manner. Therefore, about as many comets arrive a bit earlier as a bit later.

The speedup or slowdown of a comet follows much the same principle as that used for the reentry to Earth of a space shuttle. When it returns, reverse jets are fired. This slows down the shuttle enough for it to drop out of orbit; it moves in a new orbit that is closer to Earth. To slow down enough to land, the shuttle makes a series of wide S curves in the upper atmosphere. Friction with the atmosphere slows the ship (and also heats it), so it can set down smoothly on the landing strip.

COMET DUST

The tail of a comet is made up of particles that are pushed away from the nucleus when a comet is swinging around the Sun. Once the particles have been pushed away, they never return. The nucleus does not have enough gravitation to pull them in. They may remain in space spread along the comet's path for centuries. A few rain down on Earth or some other planet. Every day, some of that comet dust probably falls on you. But there's nothing to fear, since the particles are not poisonous in themselves, and they are extremely small and slow-moving.

Scientists have collected the particles from high in the atmosphere with U-2 airplanes, and scoops have found them on the ocean floor. They are much too small to be seen under an ordinary microscope. In order to look at them, one needs an electron microscope that can "see" particles smaller than a wavelength of light.

When the particles drift down to Earth, some fall on us, but most go into the ground or the sea. Each day thousands of tons of comet dust and the dust of tiny meteorites fall on our planet. Those dust particles are in the food we eat, the air we breathe, and the water we drink, but we are not aware of them.

Many of the particles that remain in space form a cloud that surrounds Earth. The cloud is illuminated by the Sun and can occasionally be observed as a faint glow in the night sky. When visible, it can be seen soon after sunset, and it fades as Earth turns into midnight.

Particles left by a comet also hang in space, spread along the comet's path. When Earth passes through that path, many of the particles are pulled to the planet. As they pass through our atmosphere, the larger particles change to gases and give off light. They are the showers of meteors, or "shooting stars," that can be seen occasionally throughout the year. (Sporadic meteors, those that appear singly and not in showers, are not comet dust.)

Early in May 1986, seven weeks after Halley's comet has passed by, Earth will enter a section of its orbit. Scien-

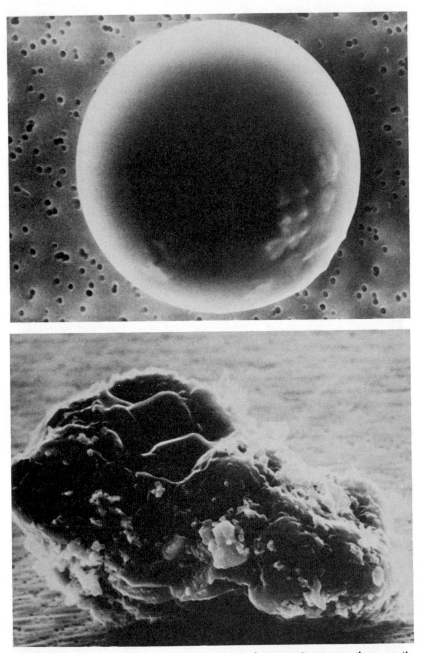

Magnified about 15,000 times by a scanning electron microscope, these particles of dust, believed shed by passing comets, may contain chemical information
dating back to the formation of the solar system 4.6 billion years ago.   NASA

Debris from Halley and other comets falls upon you. Much of it is held in space and contributes to a glow often seen in the evening.

tists expect that there will be a meteor shower. And it may be very impressive, depending on how much of Halley is lost during its journey close to the Sun.

Each year Earth goes through parts of Halley's orbit. When it does, there are meteor showers, although they are usually not spectacular. The dates of these showers, and the locations in the sky from which they seem to be coming, are on the next page.

SHOWERS	DATES	SEEM TO COME FROM	AVERAGE NUMBER PER HOUR
Eta Aquarids	May 4–6	Aquarius	20
Orionids	October 21	Orion	20

Every time a comet passes close to the Sun, it loses millions of tons of dust and gases. Very likely the comets with the longest tails lose the most material.

Eventually a comet may be reduced to nothing but solid material—all dust and gases have been pulled out of it. The chunk may remain in orbit around the Sun, or it may be captured by a planet. It may be pulled out of the solar system by a distant star. Or it may become a solid object flying through space between the orbits of Mars and Jupiter. That's the region occupied by the asteroids—solid masses ranging from pebbles to huge objects several hundred kilometers across. Very likely remains of comets are scattered here and there throughout the asteroid belt.

COMET TAILS

The tail of a comet is the part that is most apparent because it is so large. In 1986, Halley's tail may stretch for millions of kilometers and may appear to cover 30 or 40 degrees. That would be impressive, since it would mean it would extend seven or eight times the distance between the pointer stars of the Big Dipper.

Before the comet's appearance no one can be certain that the tail will be this large. It may be shorter and wider, or it may be ragged and uneven. There may even be two tails; one rather straight and the other curved. If we compare reports of ancient sightings with those of 1910 and

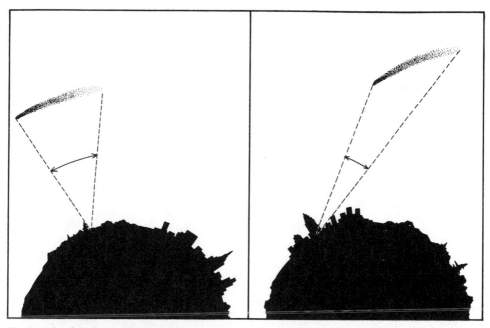

The length of Halley's tail depends upon the viewing angle. The tails here are equal in length. The one at right appears shorter because of its angle to the viewer.

1835, it seems that the tail has been growing smaller with each sighting. That would be as expected, for, as already mentioned, each time a comet passes close to the Sun, it loses millions of tons of its dust and gases.

DUST TAILS   Comets do not produce their own light; they are illuminated by the Sun as they travel near it. There are slight differences between direct sunlight and the sunlight reflected from the tail of a comet. When these differences are studied, scientists can determine what the tail is made of and how the light is produced.

Sunlight, like all light, exerts pressure. The amount is small, but in space it is enough to push free atoms and electrons. It may even be enough to push comet debris beyond the planets and out of the solar system.

As the Sun shines on particles given off by a comet's nucleus, it pushes them away, causing them to stream into space and form the tail. As they are pushed along, the particles are also lighted by the Sun. They reflect that light to us, making it possible for us to see the comet.

Whether a comet is moving toward the Sun or away from it, the pressure of sunlight is enough to thrust the small particles away from the nucleus and coma. Therefore, the tail is always pointed away from the Sun. The tail trails the comet head during the approach to the Sun, and it goes before the head as the comet moves away from the Sun. It can be compared to someone holding a flashlight so the beam is in front.

As the comet speeds around the Sun, its tail becomes curved; it does not point straight away from the Sun. The action is similar to that of a garden hose: If you swing the

When Halley is close to the Sun, a dust tail will be thrown out by the nucleus. It will curve away from the nucleus, much as water curves away from a garden hose when swung from side to side. Should Halley develop a plasma tail, it would tend to be located along the straight lines radiating from the Sun, which represent the course of the solar wind.

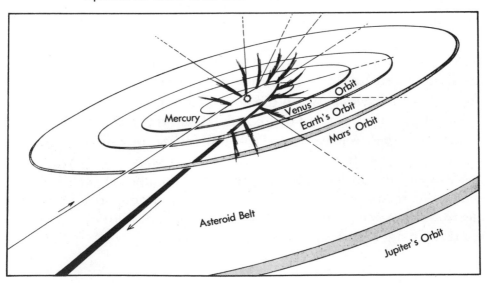

hose from right to left, the stream of water curves away. So it is with the particles thrown out by the comet.

During the visit of Halley in 1910, observers saw a section of the tail break away. The main part of the tail was made of comet dust; the part that broke away was made of plasma.

This series of photos shows changes in Halley's tail. On May 23, 1910, a section broke away, but by May 28, a new one had developed.

Mount Wilson and Las Campanas Observatories, Carnegie Institution of Washington

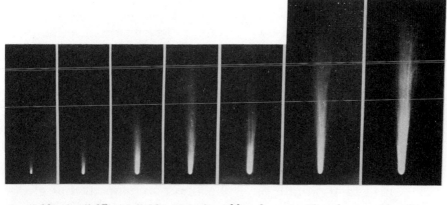

April 26 April 27 April 30 May 2 May 3 May 4 May 6

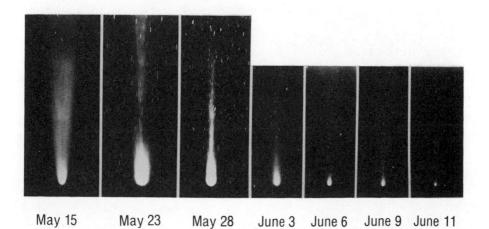

May 15 May 23 May 28 June 3 June 6 June 9 June 11

PLASMA TAILS   Every day the Sun throws a million tons of plasma—atoms that are electrically charged—into space. (Ordinarily an atom is electrically neutral. However, if it loses an electron, it carries a positive charge; if it gains an electron, it is negatively charged. In either case, the atom becomes an ion.)

Together, these ions, along with the nuclei of atoms, make up what is called the solar wind. This wind streams away from the Sun in all directions at a speed of 400 kilometers an hour. When it meets a comet, the wind reacts with the atoms in the comet's gases, changing many into ions, which become part of the plasma. Then the wind blows this plasma away from the comet head, making a tail—a plasma tail. The particles in it stream away faster and straighter than the particles in the comet's dust tail. Usually the plasma tail is also slimmer than the dust tail.

We see a dust tail because of reflected sunlight. The plasma tail is visible because of light produced by fluorescence. When you turn on a fluorescent lamp, ultraviolet radiation (which is invisible) is produced inside the tube. This radiation falls on a phosphor, a chemical that glows when it receives ultraviolet radiation. Different kinds of phosphors produce different colors, and so there are white, bluish white, and pink ultraviolet lamps. In a similar fashion, energy from the Sun is absorbed by the ions in the plasma tail. They act as a phosphor, so after a short interval the ions give off the energy in the form of visible light. Scientists know that the light in the plasma tail is given off by a variety of ions, including those of sodium, carbon, hydrogen, and oxygen.

Even though there are millions of tons of matter in a comet's dust tail, and millions of tons of ions in the plasma tail, the material is so spread out that you can see stars through the tails. There might be one speck in a volume the size of a room.

As mentioned earlier, once the particles form a tail, they are lost. During a single visit to the Sun, a comet may lose several hundred million tons of dust and vapor. During its history, Halley has probably lost a cubic kilometer of ice. No one can say how much it will lose in 1986. Providing all is not lost, however, we can be quite certain that the material left in Halley will remain intact, becoming once more a dark, cold cosmic snowball on a long journey out to the boundaries of the solar system.

5 Some Notable Comets

THE STAR OF BETHLEHEM

In 1301, Giotto di Bondone, a famous Italian painter, saw Halley's comet. Since many of his paintings concerned the life of Jesus, it occurred to him that a comet may have appeared at the time when Jesus was born. Such a comet would have been a sign of good tidings rather than one warning of disaster. And it may have been the star that the Bible mentions in Saint Matthew, chapter 2, verses 1 and 2:

Now when Jesus was born in Bethlehem of Judaea in the days of Herod the king, behold, there came wise men from the east to Jerusalem, saying, Where is he that is born King of the Jews? for we have seen his star in the east, and are come to worship him.

So strongly did Giotto think the Star of Bethlehem was a comet that he included it in his painting *The Epiphany*. The comet is clearly shown above a simple structure, beneath which are Joseph, Mary, and Jesus, and the wise men.

Although others, like Giotto, have believed that the

"star" referred to in Saint Matthew was a comet, it is very unlikely that this was the case. Halley's comet probably appeared in the fall of 12 B.C., which would have been too

In his painting *The Epiphany,* the Italian artist Giotto di Bondone suggested that the "star" the wise men followed might have been a comet.

early for people to relate the two events. And it would not have returned until about A.D. 63. Records of comets indicate that no other bright comet appeared anywhere near 6 or 7 B.C., the time when it is believed Jesus was born.

The actual identity of the star has never been determined. It may have been a bright meteor or a new star (nova) that burst into brilliance. More likely, though, the unusual sky object was a gathering together of planets. Astronomers know that during the fall of 7 B.C., and continuing into the spring of 6 B.C., Mars, Jupiter, and Saturn moved closer together as the months passed by. They made a small triangle in the constellation of Pisces, the fishes. This was significant because, centuries earlier, the same planets had appeared in that constellation just before the birth of Moses.

Not everyone would have seen the triangle, because it set before the sky had become completely dark. However, the wise men were astrologers and so would have known about the formation even if it was not easily visible. These planets may have been the sign to them that an event of great importance had occurred, and it may have been the "star" that directed their journey. We cannot be certain that this explanation is correct. However, it seems more reasonable than Giotto's belief that the object was a comet.

ENCKE'S COMET

Encke's comet, named after the German astronomer Johann Franz Encke, is notable for at least two reasons. It has made at least fifty-one orbits around the Sun, and yet, unlike most comets, it shows very little change, such as growing smaller and fainter. It also has the shortest orbital period of any of the comets, completing a journey in only 3.3 years. Halley, which takes about 75 years, is also a short-period comet.

Unfortunately most of us cannot see Encke, for it is too dim to be observed without a telescope. Astronomers who have tracked it have found that Encke does not always arrive on time. It usually is about two and a half hours early; the comet seems to be moving faster.

For a long time there was no explanation for this variation. But today scientists believe that the nucleus of Encke is spinning, and parts of its surface are heated enough to vaporize, as explained earlier on page 16. The gases are ejected, and they act as jets pushing the nucleus ahead. This speeds up the comet slightly, causing it to arrive a bit earlier than expected.

BIELA'S COMET

On February 27, 1826, a German astronomer named Wilhelm von Biela discovered a comet that became unusual because of the surprises it held. The comet may have been the same one that was seen in 1772 by the French astronomer Jacques Leibax, who called himself Montaigne of Limoges. Nevertheless, the comet was treated as a new discovery, and astronomers became interested in plotting its path.

Predictions said it would return on November 27, 1832, and it did. It arrived only twelve hours before the time that had been announced. It had a period of a mere 6.7 years, making its next appearance in 1839. However, the comet was not seen then because it moved very close to the Sun—it was in the glare of sunlight.

In 1846, the comet was seen again. On the night of January 13, Biela's comet showed the first of its surprises: The comet split apart. Apparently uneven forces in the nucleus had caused it to explode. At first the two parts were small and quite dim. But they grew rapidly in both size and brightness.

As time passed, the two comets moved farther apart, each with its own nucleus, coma, and tail. When they were about 50 000 kilometers away from each other, a light bridge seemed to connect them. Most observers think it really did not connect them, but that it was simply a tail extending from the forward half.

In 1852, when the two comets returned, they were more than 2.4 million kilometers apart. The expected visit of 1859 was not observed because, once more, the comets were in the solar glare.

The 1865 visit was anticipated with great excitement because the comets would be in good positions. But no matter how long and hard observers looked, they could not find the twin comets. They had disappeared. During their journey to the outer part of the solar system, some accident had occurred that destroyed them.

By 1872, people had lost interest in Biela's comet. But on the night of November 27, a rain of shooting stars fell from the sky. They came from the direction of the constellation Andromeda. Streaks of light came down vertically in shower after shower, with occasional blinding displays that looked like celestial fireworks. In Italy an observer counted 13,892 meteors; in England a person saw more than 10,000. No doubt the meteors were caused by particles left in the orbital path of Biela's comet. The twins must have shattered into small bits sometime after 1846, perhaps pulled apart by the gravitational pull of the outer planets or by the pull of the Sun, and the particles were strewn along the comet's path.

Every November you can still see meteor showers near Andromeda. Around the 14th, Earth encounters the region through which Biela's comet used to pass, and some of the particles come through our atmosphere. Biela's comet is no more, but its particles still affect our planet.

The same thing could happen to Halley. Stresses in the nucleus could cause it to split apart. Or it could be completely shattered by the Sun's gravitation, and clusters of the remaining particles could produce spectacular meteor showers.

DONATI'S COMET

On June 2, 1858, the Italian astronomer Giovanni Donati discovered a comet that was to become famous as one of the most beautiful comets ever seen.

Donati first saw it as a fuzzy patch. In the next few months, however, it developed a tail. In fact, it soon had several tails and was the first comet that had been observed to change in this way. At one stage, it had a long, curving tail and two straight tails. These tails stretched along a line connecting the Sun and the comet's nucleus.

As the tails developed, observers also noticed that layers were forming in the central part of the coma. These layers increased in brightness, and then decreased, sometimes disappearing altogether. As they did, other layers would appear, sometimes apparently throwing out jets of dust and gases. For the first time, observers were aware of the tremendous activity that occurs in the nucleus of a comet as it moves in closer to the Sun.

Some nine months later, Donati's comet could still be

Donati's comet over Notre Dame cathedral in Paris on October 4, 1858 as it passed near Arcturus. Notice the double tails, one curved and the other straight.

seen through a telescope. It is unusual for a comet to be visible for such a long time. Because it did not approach the Sun closely, and because of its location, the comet could be seen throughout its journey among the inner planets of the solar system.

It seems that Donati's comet has a period of some two thousand years. It may have been the same comet seen by the Chinese in 146 B.C. But it was probably not such a beautiful sight in those days as it was in 1858. The activity in the nucleus of a comet depends on its mass and its distance from the Sun. Both these conditions were likely different when the Chinese saw the comet. We can be quite sure there has been no comet before or since that could match the spectacular beauty of Donati.

COMET 1861 II

On May 13, 1861, in New South Wales, Australia, J. Tebbutt saw a comet that became memorable because of its great brightness. In fact, it was brighter than any comet seen since then, and may be the brightest ever seen from Earth. Its brightness resulted from the actual size of its nucleus and also because it moved very close to the Sun. Strangely enough, the comet has always been known by its date and number and not by the name of the person who discovered it, as is usually the case.

In those days, since there was no faster way of sending information from Australia to the rest of the world than by ship, news of the comet did not reach the Northern Hemisphere until weeks after it was first seen. There was no warning of its approach, and so on June 28, when the comet became visible in the Northern Hemisphere, it was a complete and startling surprise.

Among those who were awed by the sight was the German astronomer Johannes Schmidt. At that time he lived and worked in Athens, Greece, where he wrote this report of the comet:

On Sunday, the 30th of June at 8:30 P.M. a comet of enormous size appeared at the northwestern horizon of Athens. The twilight behind Mount Parnassus had not yet faded away when I was informed, and I can truthfully say that no other surprise could have made a deeper impression. The night before had been absolutely clear, and I had not seen a trace of the comet. Now the sky was filled by this majestic figure, spreading the tail from the horizon to beyond Polaris and even across the constellation Lyra. It was, to use the language of the past, a comet of truly fearful appearance. At 9 o'clock the head of the comet, looking as large as the moon, was next to Mount Parnassus. The head and the very wide lower part of the tail appeared like a large, distant fire, and the tail seemed like wind-blown smoke illuminated by the fire. After the head had disappeared below the horizon and it had grown dark, one could see clearly that the tail extended to the Milky Way in the constellation Aquila. At 11 P.M. I went to the observatory to watch the reappearance of the head in the northeast. At midnight and for some time after, the tail stood nearly vertically above the northern horizon, its most brilliant portion and the nucleus hidden; the tail reached 30 degrees of arc beyond the zenith. At 4:27 A.M. the head of the comet became visible again, followed by the reappearance of the brightest parts of the tail, which produced weak but noticeable shadows. Neither the Great Comet of March 1843 nor Donati's comet of October 1858 had been so bright.

I watched the rising of the comet's head with the naked eye; it was an incredible phenomenon that cannot be compared to anything else. The great mass of light hung like a dull, smoky fire over the dark outline of the mountains. As it grew lighter, the tail disappeared, I could see about 4 degrees of arc of the tail at 5:30 A.M. But at 6:08 A.M., when Capella was the only still visible star, the nucleus was still clearly luminous.

The astronomer says that the tail reached 30 degrees beyond the zenith. This means that it covered 120 degrees of the sky—truly a tremendous tail, since there are 180 degrees from horizon to horizon.

According to Schmidt, the comet was so bright that it produced shadows. This would mean that it must have been at least as bright as Venus appears when at its brightest. At such times the light is bright enough for trees and buildings to cast shadows. Comet 1861 II must have been at least magnitude −4. (That would have been very bright. Magnitude is a measure of brightness—very bright objects have minus magnitudes, dimmer objects have plus readings. The dimmest objects we can see without a telescope are sixth magnitude.) It was huge, too, according to Schmidt, as large as the full moon. What a spectacular sight it must have been.

People in the rest of the world were also excited when the comet burst, fully developed, into the sky. The cause of this was its orbit, which was steeply inclined, almost 90 degrees to the plane of Earth's orbit. Later on, Earth was to pass through the tail of the comet, and observers would see a glow over a large region of the sky.

The orbit of comet 1861 II was at an angle of almost 90 degrees to the plane of Earth's orbit.

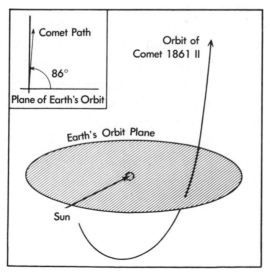

During its passage, astronomers in both Russia and Italy noticed jets spurting from the nucleus of the comet. They went out on the sunward side, then curved to become part of the tail, which appeared to be made of bundles of streaming particles.

COMET IKEYA 1963A

On January 2, 1963, a young Japanese amateur astronomer named Kaoru Ikeya detected a new comet that was well worth noticing. The story connected with its discovery is also intriguing.

When Kaoru was only six years old, he began going up on the flat roof of his house to look at the stars. During the next few years he spent time in the library, reading books about astronomy and telescope making. When he was thirteen, Kaoru decided to build his own telescope.

Kaoru and his family were doing well. Then their fortunes changed. Business at their fish store declined, making Kaoru's father despondent enough to start drinking heavily. Soon he was not able to support the family. Kaoru's mother had to go to work, and Kaoru had to leave school and get a job.

But even while the family was struggling, Kaoru kept up his interest in astronomy. He got up early to grind a mirror and to make the other parts for his telescope. By the time he was eighteen, his telescope was finished. He began to scan the skies between three and five in the mornings before he went to work.

He hoped to discover a comet. If he did, the comet would be named after Ikeya, for comets are usually named after the people who discover them. His father had disgraced the family name. If Kaoru could discover a comet, then the name Ikeya would be honored once more. It would go down in history, and whenever the comet returned, people would hear it.

On the night of January 2, 1963, Kaoru scanned the eastern sky for an hour or more. He swung his telescope to the southeast and there saw a dim object that he had noticed before. He checked his sky maps, but could find nothing on them at that location. Over and over he checked and rechecked, keeping watch on the object, and growing more and more excited.

It had to be a comet. But was it a "new" one, or one that had already been discovered and was making a return visit? As soon as it was daylight, Kaoru telegraphed information about the object to the Tokyo Astronomical Observatory. As night came, astronomers looked where Kaoru had directed, and they, too, saw the dim object. It was a comet, and it was a new one.

At nineteen, Kaoru had fulfilled a dream he had had most of his life. He had discovered a comet, and he had done it alone with a telescope he had made himself for a little over twenty dollars.

The whole world honored Kaoru Ikeya. But he did not rest on his success. Kaoru continued to survey the sky. In 1964 he found another comet, and in 1965, together with Tsutomu Seki, another amateur, he found his third comet—Ikeya–Seki 1965f. (Ikeya 1963a means the comet was the first to be found in 1963; Ikeya–Seki 1965f means the comet was the sixth to be discovered in 1965.)

There are still millions of comets waiting to be discovered. Although most are now found by professional astronomers, Kaoru's story shows that it is still possible for amateurs to find them—but they need a lot of patience.

Ikeya–Seki comet, photographed in October 1965. Kaoru Ikeya, a young Japanese astronomer, was determined to discover a comet so his family name would be respected.

COMET KOHOUTEK

Kohoutek was a comet that became well known not because of its brightness, but because it was a lot *less* bright than predicted.

Comet Kohoutek, which made an appearance in 1973, was a disappointment to the public, but a great opportunity for astronomers. These three images of comet Kohoutek were taken in November and December of 1973.   NASA

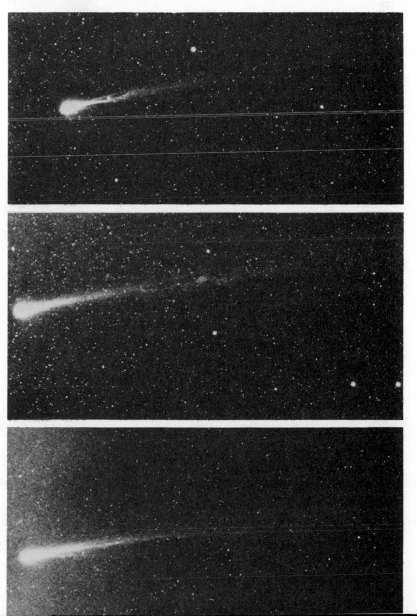

-- ⇐

The small circle represents the solar system. The orbit of comet Kohoutek is shown to the same scale. The dots are comets in the comet cloud surrounding the solar system. At some time a "nearby" star (3 meters off the page to the left) disturbed comet orbits enough to cause some comets to enter the solar system.

In March of 1973, a Czech astronomer, Lubos Kohoutek, discovered a comet while searching for asteroids on astronomical photographs. At the time of its discovery, the comet was about 688 million kilometers away, just a little closer than the orbit of Jupiter. It was very dim, but scientists reasoned that it must be an extremely large comet to be picked up at all from such a great distance.

When its orbit was studied, it was found that Kohoutek would pass close to the Sun, reaching perihelion (the closest approach to the Sun; from the Greek words *peri*, meaning near, and *helios*, the Sun) in December, some 9½ months later. Since it was a large comet, it should have become extremely bright. Astronomers had almost a year to get ready to study Kohoutek.

There was considerable excitement because Kohoutek was a "new" comet; it was making its first visit to the solar system. The journey from a thousand times farther out

Solar System

than Pluto had taken some 2 million years. Kohoutek was a collection of dust and gases that had not been contaminated during previous visits; the gases were just as they had been some 4.6 billion years ago, when Earth came into existence. By studying the comet, astronomers could learn more about the matter that existed at the time of Earth's beginning.

Kohoutek was also going to be in the best position to be highly visible in the evening skies. And because it was still far from Earth, chances were good that the comet would become spectacular as it neared the Sun. In fact, some people predicted that it would be as bright as Venus when the planet is at its brightest. That would make it next in brightness to the Moon.

Excitement about Kohoutek kept building as the time for its brightest appearance drew closer. Expeditions to view it from the sea, where the sky would be especially dark, and from ships that could move to the best latitude for viewing it, were formed. They set sail in December.

But Kohoutek never brightened enough to be seen well without using a telescope. It was a great disappointment to those who had anticipated seeing one of the wonders of the century.

Kohoutek was a great success for astronomers, though. This was the first occasion when a comet was carefully observed using instruments that had been developed over the years, such as spectrometers to analyze the light, and instruments sensitive to ultraviolet and infrared radiation. The comet could also be observed by astronauts aboard Skylab, the American space station, and by instruments aboard Mariner 10, the probe that was on its way to Venus and Mercury.

Kohoutek turned out to be a "dusty" comet, one that had dust congealed on its surface. This prevented it from vaporizing as much as was expected. And it is the vapor (or coma) around a comet nucleus that catches sunlight, making it brilliant in the twilight sky. Careful analysis of the light of Kohoutek revealed that it contained ionized water molecules, an important discovery. In addition, the comet contained hydrogen cyanide (a strong poisonous acid), methyl cyanide, carbon monoxide, and many other compounds of hydrogen, carbon, nitrogen, oxygen, and sulfur. Nine different metals, including iron and copper, were also identified.

The main part of the comet, the nucleus, which is about 30 kilometers across, is now continuing in its orbit. It will journey far beyond the solar system. Very likely it will return some 75,000 years from now, at which time it may become as bright as predicted in 1973. Possibly, though, Earth people may not see the comet again. It may be deflected from its orbit and never come close to the inner planets.

There are probably millions of comets in the outer parts of the solar system and beyond. They seem to originate in

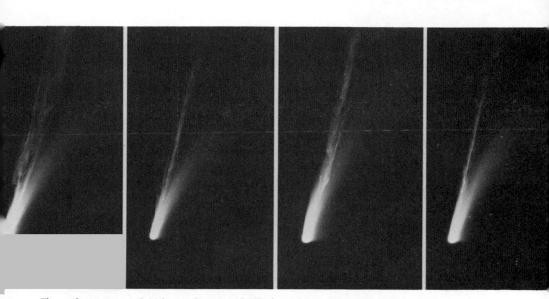

These four views of Mrkos taken in 1957 show long streamers and several changes in the comet's appearance. Palomar Observatory photograph

a vast cloud of dust and gases that surrounds the solar system. Occasionally the gases and dust come together, making a larger mass. When such a mass is deflected by the gravitation of a distant star or of the Sun, or of the outer planets, its path changes, causing the mass to move toward the inner part of the solar system. The mass has become a comet.

Each year a dozen or so of these comets are discovered. Most of them are dim and never seen except through powerful telescopes. Only astronomers know about them. But occasionally, as in the few examples mentioned here, spectacular comets appear. When they do, everyone wants to see them, because even though we know what comets are, there is still a lot of wonder attached to them.

Today, most comet discoveries are made by professional astronomers. Down through history, however, many comets were found by amateurs. A discoverer who was an amateur but who later became a professional was Caroline Herschel. In the early part of the last century, she discovered seven comets. She was the first woman to discover a comet. There may have been others before Caroline Herschel, but she was the first woman whose discoveries were entered in the records of history.

6 The Cradle of Comets

Halley travels in a flat elliptical path that extends 5 000 million kilometers out into space, which places it far beyond the orbit of Neptune. During most of its journey, the comet moves below the plane of the solar system, the imaginary surface on which the planets revolve around the Sun. Just inside the orbit of Mars, Halley rises above the plane. It sweeps around the sun and then travels once more below the plane.

We've known this only since Edmund Halley explained planetary motion after viewing the comet in 1682. Before this, people knew very little about comets. They thought they were apparitions that appeared from no one knew where, worked their evil on the Earth, and then disappeared.

It was believed that comets traveled close to Earth, much closer than the Moon, and even moved inside Earth's atmosphere. This idea persisted until 1577, when an especially bright comet appeared. It was of great interest to Tycho Brahe, a Danish astronomer who had built a large observatory equipped with the finest instruments for measuring the positions of planets, stars, and other sky objects.

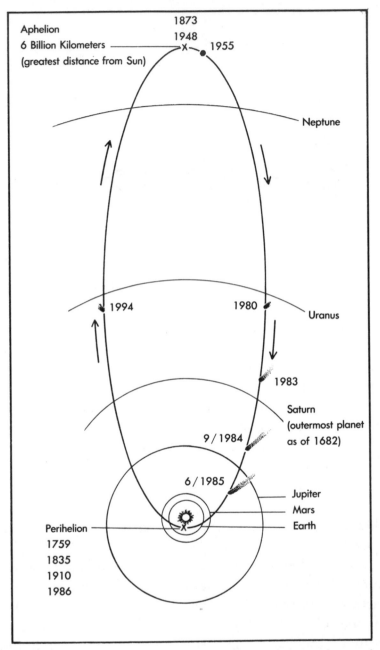

Halley moves in a flat ellipse that takes it beyond Neptune. It goes fastest when nearest the Sun. Perihelion is the orbit location nearest the Sun; aphelion is the position farthest from the Sun.

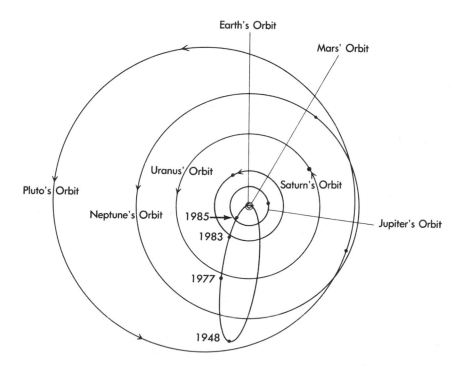

In this view from above, the orbit of Halley is seen relative to the orbits of the planets.

During most of its journey, Halley is below the solar system. It rises above it as it nears the Sun.

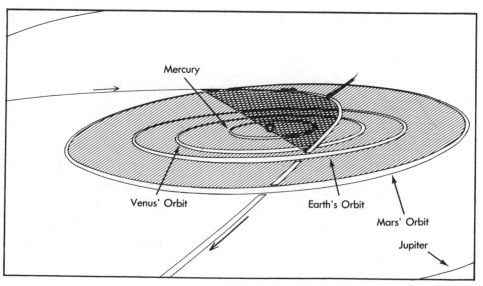

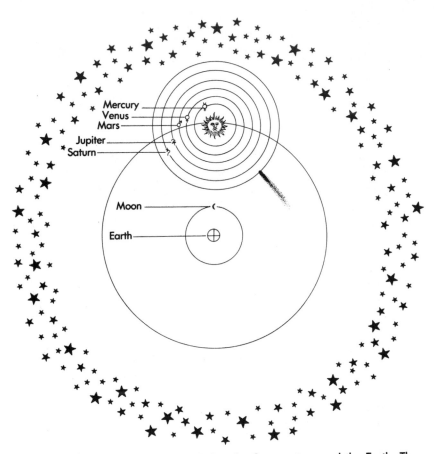

Tycho Brahe (1546–1601) believed that the Sun went around the Earth. The other planets, and comets as well, went around the Sun.

Brahe measured the comet's position from several different locations and discovered that the angles of viewing were much greater than the angles produced when viewing the Moon. Therefore, he knew that the comet had to be farther away than the Moon. Tycho concluded that comets were far off, that they probably moved around the Sun and definitely did not move through Earth's atmosphere. Brahe's observations told us a lot about the locations of comets, but did not explain where they came from.

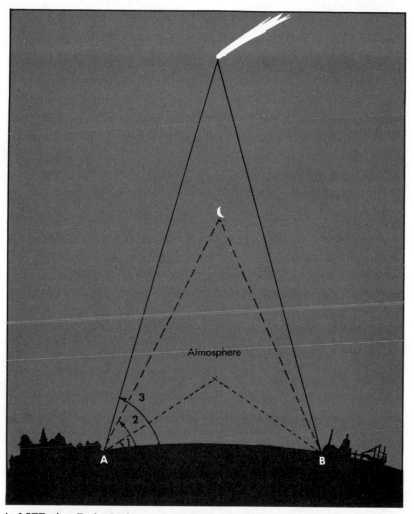

In 1577 when Tycho Brahe saw a comet, he determined that comets are beyond Earth and not, as then believed, in the atmosphere. He sighted the comet from two different locations. Because angle 3 is greater than angle 2, the comet must be farther away than the Moon.

A belief, widely accepted at that time, was that comets were thrown out by planets, that they were pieces of planetary matter that somehow spun off and traveled in separate orbits. It was further believed they were shaped like disks that traveled in straight lines.

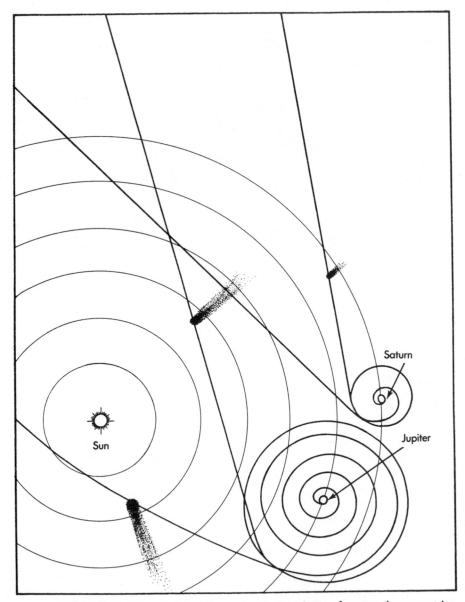

In the 1500s it was believed that comets were pieces of matter thrown out by planets. A comet spiraled out from a planet and then followed an essentially straight path across the solar system.

THE COMET-CLOUD

The belief that comets came from planets persisted for centuries. However, that changed in the 1950s when a Dutch astronomer, Jan H. Oort, who had studied the orbits of comets and had also identified many of the materials they are made of, made a startling suggestion. He supported an idea first proposed in the 1930s by the Estonian astronomer, Ernst Öpik. They believed a huge cloud which extends thousands of times farther than the outermost planets surrounds the solar system. It is composed of dust and many different substances—some that existed long before the formation of planets. If all the materials in the cloud were added together, they would comprise a mass that is only a fraction of the mass in the entire Earth. Yet this cloud contains enough material to spawn comets, perhaps a hundred billion of them or more.

Most of the particles in the comet-cloud are spread out evenly. Occasionally several particles cluster together, the mass attracts other particles, and so it continues to grow. All of the particles, including this more massive globule, are moving around the solar system. And they have been doing this for perhaps more than 4.6 billion years, the time when the solar system was formed.

At long intervals, perhaps once in a million years, a neighboring star moves in close enough to the cloud so that its gravitational force disturbs the motions of these globules. Some may be thrown out of the cloud toward these distant stars. Others may be thrown toward the inner part of the solar system and into orbits that take them close to the sun.

Some of the globules may never go into separate Sun-circling orbits. They may be captured by Jupiter, Saturn, Uranus, or Neptune, any one of the giant planets. In fact,

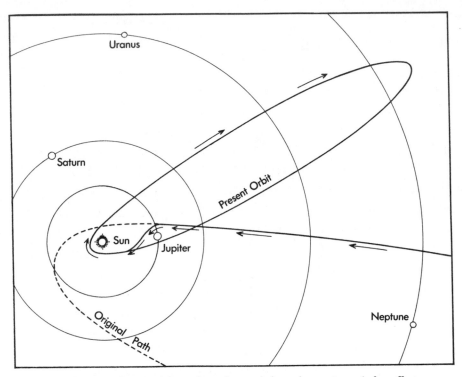

Halley may have originated out beyond the solar system. A far-off star may have deflected it toward the solar system, where the gravitational force of a planet (perhaps Jupiter) captured it and caused the comet to go into its present orbit.

some people believe that these outer planets are mainly collections of billions of comets—globules formed out of the comet-cloud that surrounds us.

HALLEY'S PREDICTION

Edmund Halley knew nothing of such ideas, but he did know about Tycho Brahe and so was aware that comets were distant objects. In 1682 he watched a comet night after night, and very carefully plotted its position and its path. He gathered a lot of information about it. After the comet had passed, Halley had several meetings with his good friend Sir Isaac Newton, who had been mulling over the motions of planets around the Sun. Data on the motions of the comet of 1682 were also studied by the two men. After long and careful analysis, Newton concluded that planets and comets moved in elliptical orbits. And

Comets travel in ellipses, parabolas, or hyperbolas. The faster the speed, the flatter the ellipse. At great speeds, the orbit becomes parabolic or hyperbolic. Comets that return move in elliptical orbits; those that appear only once move in parabolas or hyperbolas.

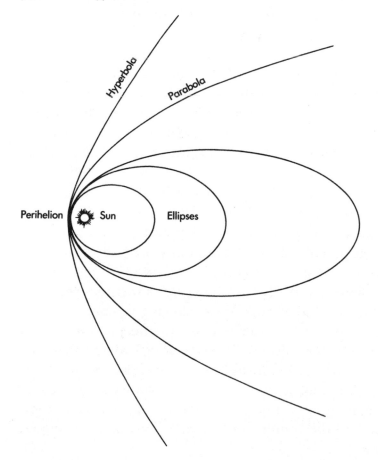

these ellipses could be very flat or very nearly perfect circles, depending on many conditions, such as speed of motion and nearness of masses with strong gravitation.

After long discussions with Newton, and after studying information available about the appearances of other comets, Halley suspected that comets did not arise spontaneously, nor did they appear and disappear in a random fashion, nor travel in straight lines. In fact, he said, comets (or at least some of them) moved in great curves and so reappeared over and over again. He believed that a comet that had appeared in 1531 and again in 1607 was the same one he saw in 1682. After turning this idea over in his mind for 23 years and discussing it with Newton, Halley wrote in 1705, "... whence I would venture confidently to predict its return (the comet of 1682) in the year 1758." This was no easy matter. In the first place, the 1682 comet had been seen during only a small part of its orbit. And in order for it to return in 1758, its orbit had to be a flat ellipse that extended far out into space, much farther than the edge of the solar system as it was then believed to be (this was before the discovery of the outer planets, Uranus, Neptune, and Pluto).

To make the prediction, Halley had to work out how much the pull of Saturn and Jupiter would affect the orbit of the comet. This was a complex matter, for the positions of the planets were always changing, sometimes speeding up the comet and at other times slowing it down. And the comet itself was sometimes close to the planets and at other times more distant. Nevertheless, Halley calculated that the comet of 1758 would be delayed by 618 days, the time required for it to complete an orbit would be a year and eight months longer than in its previous journey. Halley said the comet would reach perihelion, its closest approach to the Sun, in the middle of April 1759, give or take one month.

This was a sensational announcement because it was contradicting the general belief that comets came and went in a haphazard fashion; they arose spontaneously, and just as rapidly disappeared. Half a century after this prediction, astronomers and the public who had heard about Halley watched the skies with great care to catch the first glimpse of the "comet of 1682." They were not disappointed, for the comet passed through perihelion on March 12, 1759, one month before Halley had said it would. Unfortunately, Halley had died in 1742 and so was not able to see the return he had predicted. However, ever since that day, the comet of 1682 has been called Halley's comet, in honor of the man who first proved that comets were parts of our solar system and moved in elliptical orbits around the Sun, much as the planets do.

For perhaps three thousand years or more, Halley has been returning to our region of space every 76 years on the average. As we know, the most recent return of Halley was in 1910, when it passed through perihelion on April 20. The first photographs of it were made on September 11, 1909. From March 9, 1910, to the middle of April, it was invisible, since it was in the glare of the Sun. When it reappeared, the comet grew brighter, reaching second magnitude, which is about as bright as Polaris (the North Star) on May 10. One tail, which was visible in the hours after midnight, reached a length of 100 degrees. (There are 180 degrees from horizon to horizon.)

On May 18 the nucleus of the comet passed in front of the Sun. On May 19–21, the tail was visible before dawn, and at that time it grew to cover 140 degrees. It was then that Earth passed through the tail.

The head of Halley as it appeared on May 8, 1910. Notice the dark and bright sections in the tail as it is developing.

Mount Wilson and Las Campanas Observatories, Carnegie Institution of Washington

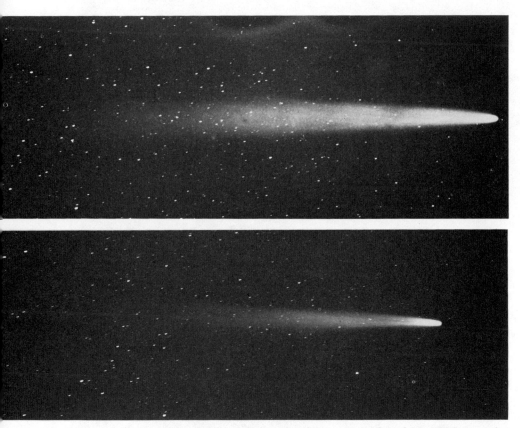

In these photos of Halley taken in Honolulu on May 12 and 15, 1910, it can be seen that changes in appearance occurred rapidly.

Mount Wilson and Las Campanas Observatories, Carnegie Institution of Washington

7 The 1986 Return of Halley

In November 1985, Halley will pass Earth on its way in toward the Sun. But it will not be visible, unless you have a telescope and know exactly where to look. By December, the comet will have become brighter and you might be able to see it after sunset with binoculars.

It probably will not be visible to the unaided eye until toward the end of January. From the Northern Hemisphere, it will be low in the western horizon after sunset, but will only be as bright as a dim star. But it will be exciting to see, especially if we keep in mind that it is the same comet seen by Caesar, King Harold, Halley, and other people of ancient days. In April it should be much brighter, when the best places for viewing it will be south of the equator.

As we get closer to 1985–1986, we can expect to hear rumors about the end of the world. During the 1835 and 1910 visits of Halley, that's what people believed was about to happen—either that, or there would be epidemics, famine, or floods that would destroy millions of people. In 1835 a woman said that the snow had turned red as blood from the comet's glare. (Perhaps there just happened to have been a red snow fall, as sometimes happens when certain spores in the atmosphere are carried to Earth by snowflakes.)

Around 1986 you may hear stories about poisons that will fall on Earth, killing off people and animals. People believed it would happen in 1910, just as they had believed it would occur whenever comets appeared. Even though people were fearful, they were excited by the 1910 visit of Halley. Stores soon ran out of telescopes; people bought them so they would get a better look at the comet.

Many people prepared for a great laugh—they would not be able to stop. They believed that when Earth went through the tail of Halley, nitrogen in our atmosphere would be changed to nitrous oxide, or laughing gas, and that people breathing it would laugh themselves to death. And if that didn't happen, they feared the comet would crash into Earth and send bolts of electricity from pole to pole, and everyone would be electrocuted.

To escape the fearful effects of the comet, people sought all sorts of "safe" places. They built solid rooms of brick, others prepared to go into mine shafts. Those who couldn't build comet sanctuaries sealed up the doors and windows of their houses to block out the poison gases. Churches were packed as the comet moved closer.

Other people were less fearful. They held comet parties or sold comet jewelry and medals celebrating the event. Some even invented "comet pills" that were to protect users from the comet, provided they took the pills regularly.

We're sure there will be comet jewelry in 1986, and also special Halley medals. Very likely comet pills of some kind will also be available to those convinced such a remedy is needed.

WHERE TO SEE HALLEY

Should you be able to travel, you'll see Halley best from Australia and New Zealand. And the best day will be April 11, 1986. At that time Halley will be closest to Earth, 60 million kilometers away. It will be in the constellation Lupus, the Wolf, southeast of Scorpius, a constellation that may be more familiar to you. (See page 65.)

Earlier, on March 7, Halley will be almost in line with the Moon. That should help you locate it. It will be in the constellation Capricornus. Before that, on February 9, Halley will be at perihelion. However, it will be on the opposite side of the Sun from us and so quite impossible to see.

Probably the best time to see Halley north of the equator will be the third week of January 1986. At that time it will be low in the western sky after sunset.

At 30° N. latitude, Halley will be visible in the evening skies of January 1986, although it will be very dim. You'll need binoculars to see it. To make them steady, hold the binoculars against a post or corner of a building. Halley will be a bit south of west. On January 25, when Halley will be brightest (mag. 3.7 which is dimmer than Polaris), it will be almost on the horizon.

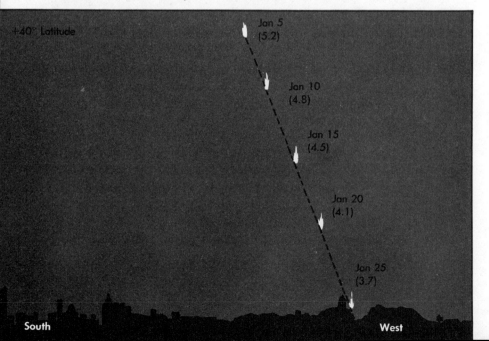

+40° Latitude

Jan 5
(5.2)

Jan 10
(4.8)

Jan 15
(4.5)

Jan 20
(4.1)

Jan 25
(3.7)

South   West

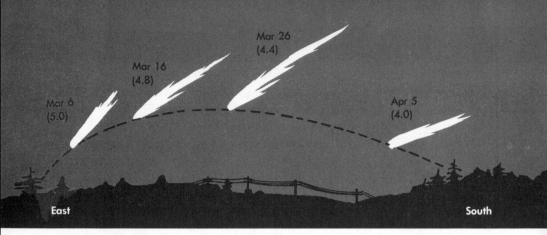

Through March 1986 and into April, Halley will be a morning object as viewed from 40° N. latitude an hour or so before sunrise. In early March it will be a bit south of east, just to the left of Sagittarius and close to the horizon. It will remain dim throughout and quite impossible to see without binoculars. The tail should be well developed.

In April 1986, Halley will be seen in the evening an hour or so after sunset. Binoculars or a small telescope will be needed to pick it up. Those with exceptional eyesight and in locations free of haze and artificial lighting may be able to discern it. It will be in the southeast just below Scorpius and moving toward Lupus and Centaurus.

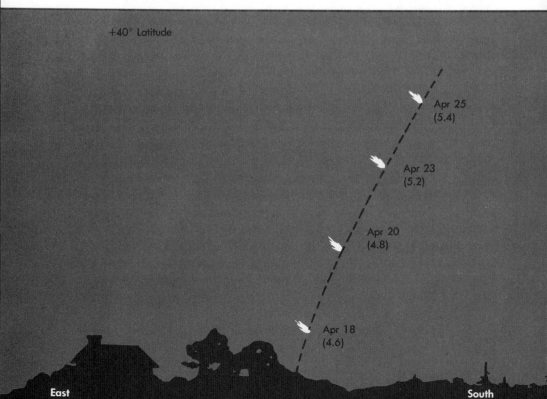

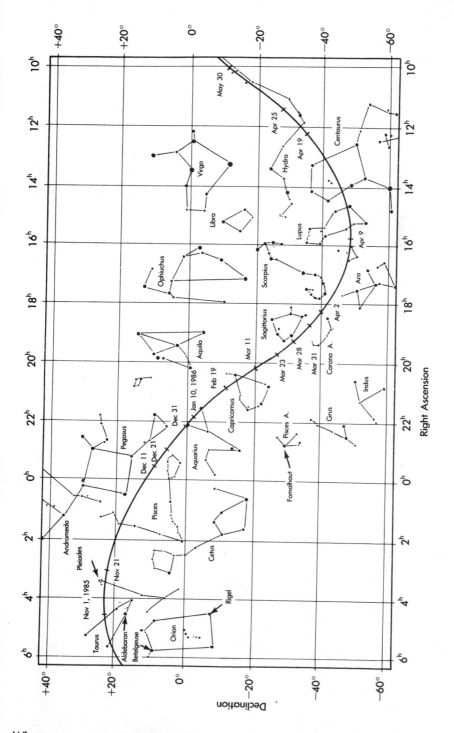

When most apparent, Halley will be south of the celestial equator. When brightest, it will be in the constellation Lupus, the Wolf, a bit below and to the right of Scorpius.

But don't expect it to be spectacular. It will probably be no brighter than a dim star. Each time a comet passes through perihelion, it loses some of the material it is made of. That's what has been happening to Halley. In 1910 it was not very bright, and it will probably be even dimmer in 1986; for with each passage, it gets a bit dimmer. According to the historical records available to them, astronomers estimate that in 243 B.C. Halley was 250 times brighter than it was in 1910.

8 International Halley Events

During recorded history, Halley has flown around the Sun 27 times. In 1910 it flew close to Earth; in fact, as mentioned earlier, we went through the comet's tail. In 1986 the comet will be farther from us. This time, in order to study it well, we must go out to it, which is something we can do with space probes. There will not be another opportunity until 2061.

This is the first time that scientists will have a chance to observe a comet from spacecraft. Since the comet's orbit can be determined accurately, a craft can be aimed to intercept and be correct within a hundred kilometers or so. So far, our best information about the makeup of comets was obtained in 1973, when Kohoutek circled the Sun. But much more detailed study is now possible during the appearance of Halley.

It is hoped that the United States will send a probe to Halley. Concise plans for one have been drawn up. At the time this is written, however, funds for the mission have not been approved by Congress.

If the funds are made available, the Halley Intercept Mission will be centered on a probe designed to survey all parts of the comet; the nucleus, which is only a few kilo-

The Halley intercept vehicle is derived from the Voyagers, the Galileo orbiter, and the Viking spacecraft. It is a cluster of instruments for studying Halley and transmitting information back to Earth.   Jet Propulsion Laboratory

meters across, the extensive coma of gases and dust surrounding the nucleus, and the tail of very thin gases.

The vehicle—if approved—will be launched in the summer of 1985, setting out on a journey of about eight months. It will be carried into low-Earth orbit aboard a space shuttle. Once in orbit, the interceptor, mounted on the head of a solid-rocket booster, will be lifted out of the shuttle. After separation, the rocket will be fired. Then the rocket and interceptor will separate and the interceptor will enter a flight path around the Sun, one that will take it close to Halley.

About six months into the mission, cameras aboard the interceptor will begin photographing the comet, sending about three thousand pictures back to Earth. They will show the tail and coma in considerable detail, both because of the nearness of the interceptor to Halley and because there will be no disturbing atmosphere, as there is on Earth.

As the interceptor moves in closer, the cameras will continue to send back photographs, each series being a bit more detailed because of the shortening distance. Three hours before its closest approach, the probe will plunge into Halley's cloud of dust and gases in the region of the coma. The comet and the probe will be moving toward each other at a velocity of some 200 000 kilometers an hour. At that speed, the dust particles could cause serious damage to the camera and transmitters, so the interceptors instruments will be protected by a large shield that will deflect the particles.

While speeding into the coma, the probe will measure the gas and dust concentration as it "boils" off the nucleus. The cameras will continue to function, though it might be like taking pictures inside a cloud.

As it closes in, the craft will be only about 800 kilometers from the nucleus and will still be taking pictures. Ten days after the encounter, the mission will be over. The interceptor will continue in its orbit around the Sun, an orbit closely matching that of Earth. Halley will also go around the Sun, but its orbit is a flat ellipse, so it will go out beyond Jupiter.

THE EUROPEAN SPACE AGENCY

Even if the Halley Intercept Mission does not fly, other Halley probes will be sent out by European countries, and by the Soviet Union and Japan.

Many Western European countries have joined together to form ESA, the European Space Agency. They

The European Space Agency will launch a probe, called Giotto, in the summer of 1985.   European Space Agency

plan to launch a Halley probe, which is being called Giotto after the Italian painter mentioned earlier.

Giotto will be a three-quarter-ton cylinder containing all kinds of measuring instruments, including cameras, devices to determine the kinds of gases in the comet, ultraviolet detectors, thermometers, and electric-charge measurers. It will begin its journey in the summer of 1985, and by March 1986 it will plunge into the dense dust of Halley

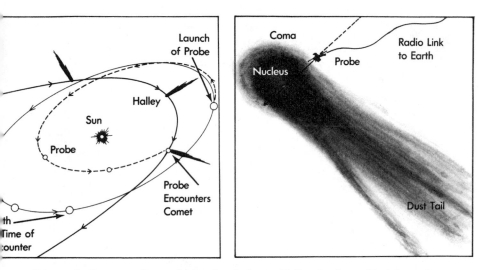

Giotto, the European Space Agency's mission to Halley, is planned to intercept the comet on March 17, 1986. The probe will go through the coma and approach the nucleus.

at a speed of some 245 000 kilometers an hour. As it does, the probe will gather data and send them back to Earth-based receivers. At that velocity, friction with the particles that make up Halley will heat Giotto and perhaps erode it rapidly, so the craft will not last very long. Therefore, it will send its information directly to Earth rather than storing it for later transmission.

RUSSIA AND JAPAN

The Giotto mission is a certainty, and plans are moving along for the construction of the probe and for its voyage.

In addition, the Soviet Union will probably modify the course of one, or perhaps two, of its Venus probes so that they will move within about 10 000 kilometers of Halley. Very likely the Russian probes will carry advanced devices, such as cameras to take pictures in visible light as well as ultraviolet, thermometers to measure temperature,

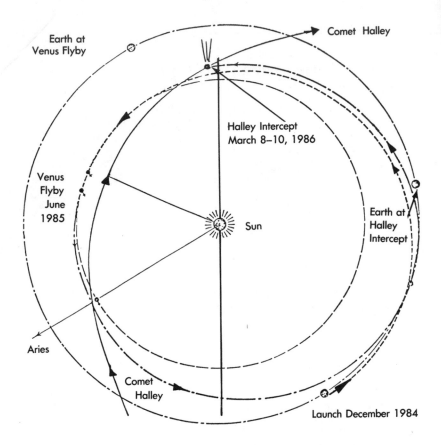

The Russians may modify one of their Venus missions so it will intercept Halley. Launched in 1984, it would fly by Venus in 1985, and intercept Halley in March 1986.

Science News

instruments to determine the number of ions and the electric charges on them, and the amount of dust and size of the particles.

It is also likely that Japan will develop a probe and send it out to the nucleus of Halley. Its main purpose will be to measure ultraviolet radiation in that region. No cameras are planned because they add a lot of weight, and the other countries will probably make their photographs available to people who want them.

INTERNATIONAL HALLEY WATCH

It is hoped that all the Halley probes that are in the planning stage will be launched in the summer of 1985 (the Russian probe would be launched earlier, in December 1984). But even if they are not, Halley will still be the most intensely studied of any comet. Right now a telescope 96 inches in diameter is being prepared for launching into space in 1985. It will be carried aloft aboard a space shuttle. Although the instrument is smaller than many Earth-based telescopes, it will be much more powerful. Since it will operate in the utter blackness of space, there will be no atmosphere to distort and dim the images. The space telescope will be able to see Halley very well, and it will send the information it gathers back to Earth.

In addition to the space telescope, there are many improved satellite- and ground-based instruments available that we did not have in 1910, or even in 1973, when Kohoutek made its visit. There are supersensitive radio telescopes, and telescopes that are sensitive to X rays and gamma rays, as well as to ultraviolet radiation. These instruments can "see" features of Halley that are not perceptible in visible light.

Astronomers around the world will be concentrating on Halley. In order to coordinate their efforts, prevent unnecessary duplication, and be certain that all aspects of Halley are investigated, the International Halley Watch has been set up. Its center will be the Jet Propulsion Laboratory of the University of California in Pasadena. The Watch will continue for eight years. It will spend several years preparing for Halley, monitor the approach itself, and follow up by studying the data gathered.

Scientists from many countries will gather information about Halley—its appearance, what it is made of, activity of the nucleus, coma, and tail, and the motion of the comet. All the findings will go to the center, where they will be assembled and organized. Once the information is in order, it will be made available to scientists, students, and teachers.

As 1986 approaches, people everywhere will search the skies for a glimpse of Halley. But not everyone will be watching the skies; some will seek shelter from the dangers they think it will bring.

Don't get caught up in comet hysteria. But do be sure to see Halley, just as millions of people have throughout history, including Edmund Halley himself in 1682.

Let's hope for clear skies and good viewing.

Further Reading

Anderson, Norman D., and Brown, Walter R. *Halley's Comet.* New York: Dodd, Mead, 1981.

Brandt, John C., ed. *Comets.* Readings from *Scientific American.* San Francisco: W. H. Freeman, 1981.

Branley, Franklyn M. *Comets, Meteoroids and Asteroids.* New York: T. Y. Crowell, 1974.

Brown, Peter L. *Comets, Meteorites and Men.* New York: Taplinger, 1974.

Brownlee, Donald E. "Cosmic Dust." *Natural History Magazine,* April 1981.

Calder, Nigel. *The Comet is Coming.* New York: Viking, 1980.

Ley, Willy. *Visitors from Afar: The Comets.* New York: McGraw-Hill, 1969.

NASA. *Halley's Comet: A Unique Opportunity in Space Exploration.* Pasadena: California Institute of Technology, Jet Propulsion Laboratory, 1981.

————. *International Halley Watch.* Pasadena: California Institute of Technology, Jet Propulsion Laboratory, 1981.

————. *Journey to Halley's Comet.* Pasadena: California Institute of Technology, Jet Propulsion Laboratory, 1981.

Oppenheimer, Michael. "What Are Comets Made Of?" *Natural History Magazine,* March 1978.

Oppenheimer, Michael, and Haimson, Leonie. "The Comet Syndrome." *Natural History Magazine,* December 1980.

Ronan, Colin A. *Edmund Halley: Genius in Eclipse.* New York: Doubleday, 1969.

Whipple, Fred. "The Nature of Comets." *Scientific American,* February 1974.

————. "The Spin of Comets." *Scientific American,* March 1980.

Yeomans, Donald K. *The Comet Halley Handbook.* Pasadena: NASA, California Institute of Technology, Jet Propulsion Laboratory, 1981.

Index

Page numbers in *italics* refer to illustrations.

Twain, Mark (Samuel Clem-
ens), 2

ultraviolet radiation, 26
Uranus, 16, *48, 54*
   comet-cloud and, 53–54
   orbit of, 49

Venus, 37, *50*
   orbit of, *24, 49*

Venus probes, 71–72, *72,* 73
Virgo, *65*

wars, comets associated with,
   3–6, *9*
water:
   in comet Kohoutek, 44
   in comet nucleus, 15
Wesley, John, 10, 12
William I, king of England, 3

About the Author

FRANKLYN M. BRANLEY is the author of many outstanding books for young people on astronomy and other sciences, including *Space Colony* and *Jupiter.* He is Astronomer Emeritus and former chairman of The American Museum–Hayden Planetarium.

He says, "This book comes out of decades of interest in all aspects of astronomy. Although we know that comets do not foretell earthly events—they are little more than cosmic snowballs—they still intrigue us. Halley's comet is of special interest because of its many return trips—and because it opened the way toward our modern understanding of comets."

Dr. Branley and his wife live in Sag Harbor, New York.